T0131763

LIVING YOUR BLESSED LIFE
THE TRUTH WILL
SET YOU FREE

VOLUME 1

JUSTIN A. DAVIS

authorHOUSE®

AuthorHouse™
1663 Liberty Drive
Bloomington, IN 47403
www.authorhouse.com
Phone: 1 (800) 839-8640

Published by AuthorHouse   04/03/2020

ISBN: 978-1-7283-5095-0 (sc)
ISBN: 978-1-7283-5094-3 (e)

Library of Congress Control Number: 2020904928

Print information available on the last page.

CONTENTS

WELCOME TO YOUR TRUTH

This workbook is designed to take you on a spiritual journey in search of your TRUTH. God's TRUTH will be at the forefront of this journey, but just as important, we must find your TRUTH for God's purpose to manifest completely in your life.

You will be challenged to reflect on what you've learned throughout your life thus far, remember past events that have changed you for better or worse, accept those things you cannot go back and change, and to forgive yourself for things you may have done in the past to hurt yourself or the people you love.

Over the next 8 weeks, this course will focus on different aspects of TRUTH chronicled by the infallible Word of God. The goal is to find your TRUTH in relation to God's intended TRUTH.

To get the maximum results from this workbook, I suggest you set aside

10-15 minutes a day to study and reflect.

Every week we will focus on a different aspect of TRUTH, and you will have daily exercises assigned to you. After completing this book, you will know God's TRUTH and God willing, you will find your TRUTH as well.

DAILY EXERCISES:

1. **My Powerful Affirmation's**

One thing we must do is renew our thinking and speaking if we want to change our lives for the better. Every thought you think and every word you speak is an affirmation. You're using affirmations every moment whether you know it or not.

Use the worksheets provided in the back of the workbook, to create an affirmation each day except Sunday. At the end of your 8-week journey, you will have a list of 48 powerful affirmations that will empower you. This list of affirmations will be a resource you can return to when the struggles of life begin to weigh heavy on your spirit. To be proactive and stay in the right state of mind, I suggest reading them daily. The bible speaks of transforming and renewing our minds, what better way to do it than this?

2. **My Gratitude Jar**:

A Gratitude Jar provides a simple way of being reminded of all the things that you are grateful for. Every day write down one thing you're grateful for and put it in the jar. On days when you're feeling doubt or you just need confirmation of how great GOD is and how great YOU are since you were created in his image, simply read one of your entries.

*Find a jar to decorate and personalize it anyway you like.

WEEK 1-DAY 1

(What is God's TRUTH about you?)

John 15:1-5 (NIV Translation)

15 *"I am the true vine, and my Father is the gardener.* *²He cuts off every branch in me that bears no fruit, while every branch that does bear fruit he prunes[a] so that it will be even more fruitful.* *³You are already clean because of the word I have spoken to you.* *⁴Remain in me, as I also remain in you. No branch can bear fruit by itself; it must remain in the vine. Neither can you bear fruit unless you remain in me.*

⁵"I am the vine; you are the branches. If you remain in me and I in you, you will bear much fruit; apart from me you can do nothing.

God's truth and your truth may be two very different realities. For those that don't know my story, my mother had 4 children by 4 different men by the age of 24. She had my older brother at 18, me at 21, my sister at 22, and my baby sister at 24. I was born into extreme poverty, where domestic violence and alcoholism were simply a way of life. I'd have to use all my fingers and toes plus borrow some of yours to count how many different apartments and houses I had to call home before the age of 18. I've even experienced homelessness due to my family dynamic early in life. Hearing a story like this, most people would assume that any child exposed to these circumstances would end up in dire straits. But, the TRUTH of the matter is that God, had his hand on my life the entire time. He healed my stepfather of alcoholism and he became the greatest Dad I could ask for. I went to college on a full-academic scholarship. I even got a chance to live my dream of playing college basketball and becoming a teacher all before the age of 24. You see, I had a praying mother who believed that no matter what, God would take care of her and her children. She taught me early that God's WORD was the TRUTH, and God's Word would protect me no matter what challenges life would bring. Throughout my life, she and a few others pushed me towards God and his WORD and because of it, eventually I fully committed to serving God at the age of 25. Once I committed, God's word (TRUTH) changed my life for forever.

The scriptures in the bible opened my eyes to the TRUTH, about who I was as a Christian, my gifts, talents, and where I stood as a child of God. I began studying. And God began speaking to my heart.

This is what God whispered to me:

You are chosen. You are loved. You are holy. You are worthy.

You can do all things through Christ.

God continues to challenge me to see myself as he sees me. I've only been able to do this by embracing God's TRUTH which is only found in his WORD. And that's what I'm challenging you to do today: Let go of your insecurities. Let go of the baggage that may be holding you down. What do you need to change in your life in order to be truly happy? I need you to be honest with yourself and take hold of your TRUTH. Take your place and stand in your true greatness.

1. List 3 TRUE statements that you talk to God about all the time that you know you need his help changing.

_____

_____

_____

_____

_____

_____

_____

<u>Daily Assignment:</u>

- Write your Daily Affirmation on **My Powerful Affirmation's** pages in the back.
- Write down one thing you are grateful for and place in your **My Gratitude Jar.**

Justin A. Davis

WEEK 1-DAY 2

(I AM CREATED IN GOD'S IMAGE)

You were created in God's image. Let that sink in for a minute. The creator of the universe decided to make everything else you see on the planet and he chose to make you in his own image. I really don't think most of us understand how special we are. There are millions of God's living creations, yet you and I were created in his image.

This means we are creative, powerful, merciful, intelligent.... I could go on and on. God's spirit is our spirit and there is no separation between us.

Answer the following question TRUTHFULLY.

Does the image that you display to the people around you, show the image of God as you see him?

If there was 1 thing you could change right now that would help people see more of God in you, what would it be and how can you change it?

_____

_____

_____

_____

_____

*What does God say about being created in HIS IMAGE?

Genesis 1:27-So God created man in his own image, in the image of God he created him; male and female he created them. (NIV Translation)

What do you think God means when he says, "He made Man in his own Image?" Support your answer with at least 1 scripture from the Bible.

_____

_____

_____

_____

_____

_____

_____

_____

_____

Daily Assignment:

- Write your Daily Affirmation on **My Powerful Affirmation's** pages in the back.
- Write down one thing you are grateful for and place in your **My Gratitude Jar.**

WEEK 1-DAY 3

(I AM VALUABLE)

We learned yesterday that God created us in his own image. Now that we know this, is there any doubt just how valuable you are? What can be worth more than God? You were born to be the most intelligent being in God's creation. Think about other forms of life. I'm pretty sure if you could choose what you wanted to be; you would've chosen to be a human being. You are blessed and God created all of us with so much value. If you can't see that, then we've got a lot of work to do

Answer the following question TRUTHFULLY.

Do you feel as valuable as God sees you? Whether you answer yes or no explain why.

_____

_____

_____

_____

_____

_____

_____

_____

*What does God say about your VALUE?

Isaiah 43:4-Since you are precious and honored in my sight, and because I love you, I will give people in exchange for you, nations in exchange for your life. (NIV Translation)

On a scale of 1 to 10, how valued do you feel? On a scaled of 1 to 10 what Value do you believe God would give you. Support your answer with a factual reason.

_____

_____

_____

_____

_____

_____

_____

_____

_____

_____

Daily Assignment:

- Write your Daily Affirmation on **My Powerful Affirmation's** pages in the back.
- Write down one thing you are grateful for and place in your **My Gratitude Jar.**

Justin A. Davis

WEEK 1-DAY 4

(I AM CHOSEN)

Being chosen always feels good. As children it would always feel good to get chosen to be a part of a team or be chosen by the teacher to be the helper. Even in our adult years it still feels pretty good to be chosen. God chose us to have dominion over the earth. God also chose us to be fellow heirs with his son Jesus. Have you ever stopped to think for a second why he chose us and made us so special in comparison to everything else on the planet?

Answer the following question TRUTHFULLY.

Do you feel like a chosen child of God? When was the last time you felt fully connected to God?

_____

_____

_____

_____

_____

_____

_____

_____

_____

_____

*What does GOD say about you being CHOSEN?

I Peter 2:9-But you are a chosen race, a royal priesthood, a holy nation, God's special possession, that you may declare the praises of him who called you out of darkness into his wonderful light. (NIV Translation)

What 2 qualities do you possess that makes you believe that God chose <u>YOU</u> for a greater purpose? Explain why you feel this way.

_____

_____

_____

_____

_____

_____

_____

_____

<u>Daily Assignment:</u>

- Write your Daily Affirmation on **My Powerful Affirmation's** pages in the back.
- Write down one thing you are grateful for and place in your **My Gratitude Jar.**

Justin A. Davis

WEEK 1-DAY 5

(I AM NEW CREATION)

Have you ever bought something new? I mean, brand new like nobody else has come close to owning it. If so, then you know what it feels like to have something new in your possession. As humans we have an ability that no other species has. We have the ability to think and change our mind if we choose. In essence, we might be the only entity on the planet that can literally become a new creation whenever we are ready.

Answer the following question TRUTHFULLY.

When, if ever, have you felt like a new creation? Why is it so difficult for people to change their ways?

_____

_____

_____

_____

_____

_____

_____

*What does GOD say about you being a NEW CREATION?

2 Corinthians 5:17-Therefore, if anyone is in Christ, the new creation has come; The old has gone, the new is here! (NIV Translation)

What are the 2 most dominant things that you have changed about yourself since you have become a New Creation? How do you feel about this accomplishment, and how has it helped you be a better person?

_____

_____

_____

_____

_____

_____

_____

_____

_____

_____

Daily Assignment:

- Write your Daily Affirmation on **My Powerful Affirmation's** pages in the back.
- Write down one thing you are grateful for and place in your **My Gratitude Jar.**

WEEK 1-DAY 6

(I WAS A SINNER)

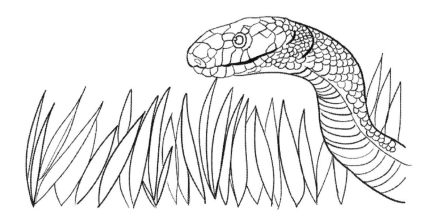

There is no such thing as a perfect man. Every single person that has ever walked and will ever walk the face of this earth will have this lack of perfection in common. Not only are we and will we be imperfect, sometimes we can be just unbearably mean-spirited. The great thing though, is that there is a cure for it. We don't have to go through our lives' hoping that things will change for the better. We have been given the power to take control of our life if we simply acknowledge that we need help and are willing to follow God's teachings.

Answer the following question TRUTHFULLY.

Sin is something that most of us try to hide. What sin have you committed in the past that you are most ashamed of and why?

_____

_____

_____

_____

_____

_____

_____

_____

*What does GOD say about being a sinner?

Ecclesiastes 7:20-Indeed, there is no one on earth who is righteous, no one who does what is right and never sins. (NIV Translation)

If God knows that you were a sinner, what made him love you so much? Support your answer with at least 1 scripture from the Bible.

_____

_____

_____

_____

_____

_____

_____

_____

_____

_____

_____

_____

_____

Daily Assignment:

- Write your Daily Affirmation on **My Powerful Affirmation's** pages in the back.
- Write down one thing you are grateful for and place in your **My Gratitude Jar.**

Justin A. Davis

Day 7 Reflecting on My Truth

For the last 6 days you have written down daily affirmations.

For this next exercise, I want you to go through your affirmations and rate them on a scale of 1 to 3.

<u>Rate Number</u>

1 = Living in My Truth
2 = Kind of Living in My Truth
3 = Currently not living in my Truth.

A. Choose an affirmation that is currently closest to your **TRUTH**. Give an example of how you are living that truth.

_____

_____

_____

_____

_____

_____

_____

_____

B. Choose an affirmation that is currently furthest from your **TRUTH.** Give an example of how you will take steps into making that your **TRUTH.**

_____

_____

_____

_____

_____

_____

_____

WEEK 2

What is Your Truth?

1 John 1:8-10 (NIV Translation)

If we claim to be without sin, we deceive ourselves and the truth is not in us. If we confess our sins, he is faithful and just and will forgive us our sins and purify us from all unrighteousness. If we claim we have not sinned, we make him out to be a liar and the word is not in us.

During my college years, life threw me a lot of curve balls and I swung at all of them. I hit a few, but the truth is I missed a lot too. I did more than the typical college student because I was in a fraternity and a basketball player so the fame and notoriety that I got made it difficult to stay humble. The Word of God says that "Pride" comes before a fall and it's hard not to become prideful when so many people are praising you. That praise led to me making a lot of dumb decisions that led to a lot of pain.

This week's lesson is about accepting YOUR TRUTH. My TRUTH was that my family was extremely poor growing up and due to this fact, I got teased a lot. So, when I got an opportunity to be praised or even worshipped by others during my college years it made me feel like I was worthy. I didn't realize that my early childhood pain left me vulnerable to wanting validation from others. I knew the things that I was doing wasn't' right, but I was receiving so much praise from others it was addictive. I knew I needed a change in my life and luckily God began to work on me. My life changed when I took a good look in the mirror and saw where I was in my life. My life changed forever when I accepted my TRUTH. My TRUTH was that I was living a life of sin because I was afraid that if I didn't, the notoriety that I had gained might somehow fade away.

Daily Assignment:

- Write your Daily Affirmation on **My Powerful Affirmation's** pages in the back.
- Write down one thing you are grateful for and place in your **My Gratitude Jar.**

WEEK 2-DAY 2

(PRIDE vs. HUMILITY)

Pride is a tough word to discuss. It's one of those words that sort of has 2 meanings. I've heard people say, "I see you take so much pride in what you do," and it means something good. I've also heard people say, "You know that pride comes before a fall," and that's not good at all. So, for today's activity instead of focusing on pride let's focus on humility.

Answer the following question TRUTHFULLY.

Do you believe "Humility" is a good thing? Be honest with yourself by explaining and giving an example why you feel the way you do.

_____

_____

_____

_____

_____

_____

Justin A. Davis

*What does GOD say about HUMILITY?

James 4:6-But he gives us more grace. That is why the scripture says, "God opposes the proud but shows favor to the humble. (NIV Translation)

After comparing your view of yourself regarding Humility to God's view of Humility, explain what changes if any you are willing to make?

_____

_____

_____

_____

_____

_____

_____

_____

_____

_____

_____

_____

_____

Daily Assignment:

- Write your Daily Affirmation on **My Powerful Affirmation's** pages in the back.
- Write down one thing you are grateful for and place in your **My Gratitude Jar.**

WEEK 2-DAY 3

(GREED vs. SHARING)

Today's society is driven by a me-first mentality in everything that we do. Is it any wonder that greed is running rampant? Greed is a major contributor to poverty. Although the bible teaches that the poor will always be with us, that doesn't mean that he's ok with us being greedy. Today, let's take some time to think about whether we are part of the greed community or the sharing community.

Answer the following question TRUTHFULLY.

Do you have a hard time sharing the blessings that God has given you? Whether you answer yes or no, explain yourself and give an example to support your comment.

_____

_____

_____

_____

_____

_____

_____

_____

_____

*What does GOD say about SHARING?

Hebrews 13:16-And do not forget to do good and to share with others, for with such sacrifices God is pleased. (NIV Translation)

After comparing your view of yourself regarding Sharing to God's view of Sharing, explain what changes if any are you willing to make?

_____

_____

_____

_____

_____

_____

_____

_____

_____

_____

_____

_____

Daily Assignment:

- Write your Daily Affirmation on **My Powerful Affirmation's** pages in the back.
- Write down one thing you are grateful for and place in your **My Gratitude Jar.**

WEEK 2-DAY 4

(LUST vs. SELF-DISCIPLINE)

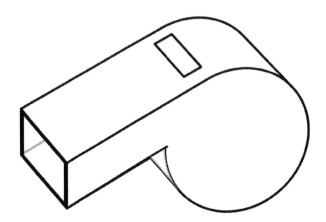

If you really think about it, most of the bible is trying to teach us 2 things. The first things it's trying to teach us, is how to love God and ourselves. The second thing it's trying to teach us, is how to love our neighbor. This doesn't sound too difficult, but apparently it is. That's why thousands of years after the death of Christ, it is still the bestselling book of all-time. So many of us struggle with controlling our feelings. It's so easy to give into the negative feelings that cause us to hurt ourselves or others. Today, let's be truthful about our level of self-discipline.

Answer the following question TRUTHFULLY.

Do you find it difficult to stop yourself from doing things that you know are harmful to you or others when you get in your feelings? If so, give an example and if not, explain what you do to prevent it from happening.

_____

_____

_____

_____

_____

_____

_____

_____

Justin A. Davis

*What does GOD say about SELF-DISCIPLINE?

Proverbs 16-32-Better a patient person than a warrior, one with self-control than one who takes the city. (NIV Translation)

After comparing your view of yourself regarding Self-Discipline to God's view of Self-Discipline, explain what changes if any are you willing to make?

_____

_____

_____

_____

_____

_____

_____

_____

_____

_____

_____

Daily Assignment:

- Write your Daily Affirmation on **My Powerful Affirmation's** pages in the back.
- Write down one thing you are grateful for and place in your **My Gratitude Jar.**

WEEK 2-DAY 5

(ENVY vs. CONTENTMENT)

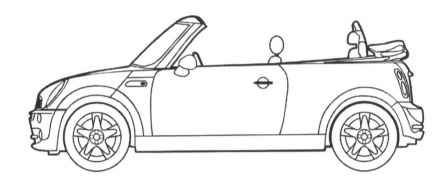

We've all been there before. Looking at someone who seems to have it all together. We secretly wish our lives were a little less like our own and more like that someone else's. Remember, this book is about truth. You can act like you've never done it, but if you are honest you know that you have. Everybody is different. Maybe you wanted a car you saw your boss driving. Maybe you wanted the watch you saw your friend wearing. Better yet, maybe you wished your friend's girl was your girl or man was your man. We've all been there at some time. Today, let's be real with ourselves about the things we envy others for.

Answer the following question TRUTHFULLY.

What is the 1 thing if any, you envy of a family member or friend currently? If you had to trade 1 thing about your life, for 1 thing in another person's life, what would it be and why?

_____

_____

_____

_____

_____

_____

_____

_____

What does GOD say about CONTENTMENT?

1 Timothy 6:6-7-But godliness with contentment is great gain. For we brought nothing into the world, and we can take nothing out of it. (NIV Translation)

After reading God's view of Contentment, should you be content with your current circumstance? Explain your answer.

_____

_____

_____

_____

_____

_____

_____

_____

_____

_____

Daily Assignment:

- Write your Daily Affirmation on **My Powerful Affirmation's** pages in the back.
- Write down one thing you are grateful for and place in your **My Gratitude Jar.**

WEEK 2-DAY 6

(ANGER vs. PEACE)

Anger is a natural emotion that we all feel. Sometimes anger can even evoke change for the better. More times than not though, it pushes us to a point that we stop thinking logically and we end up doing something that we regret later. Anger is one of those things that can consume you before you realize it. We have all fallen victim to its lure. I've come to believe that for some of us, sometimes it just feels good to be angry. The only problem is, that if we allow this to happen too often it becomes part of our character and we just can't turn the switch off.

Answer the following question TRUTHFULLY.

What is the last thing you allowed yourself to get really angry about? Now that you have thought about the incident, was the issue that made you angry ever resolved? Why or Why not?

_____

_____

_____

_____

_____

_____

_____

　　　　　　　　Justin A. Davis

*What does God say about Peace?

2 Thessalonians 3:16- Now may the Lord of peace himself give you peace at all times in every way. (NIV Translation)

In what area of your life do you currently need Peace the most? Write a prayer of peace for this area and say it every night until God gives you peace.

_____

_____

_____

_____

_____

_____

_____

_____

_____

_____

Daily Assignment:

- Write your Daily Affirmation on **My Powerful Affirmation's** pages in the back.
- Write down one thing you are grateful for and place in your **My Gratitude Jar.**

Day 7 Reflecting on My Truth

For the last 6 days you have written down daily affirmations.

For this next exercise, I want you to go through your affirmations and rate them on a scale of 1 to 3.

<u>Rate Number</u>

1 = Living in My Truth
2 = Kind of Living in My Truth
3 = Currently not living in my Truth.

C. Choose an affirmation that is currently closest to your **TRUTH**. Give an example of how you are living that truth.

_____

_____

_____

_____

_____

_____

D. Choose an affirmation that is currently furthest from your **TRUTH.** Give an example of how you will take steps into making that your **TRUTH.**

_____

_____

_____

_____

_____

Justin A. Davis

WEEK 3

The Truth Will Set Your Free

John 8 31 (NIV Translation)

31 To the Jews who had believed him, Jesus said, "If you hold to my teaching, you are really my disciples. 32 Then you will know the truth, and the truth will set you free."

What was my TRUTH? My TRUTH was that I loved the mother of my child, but she hurt me so much that I did things that I knew would hurt her because she had hurt me. I know some of you all reading might not be willing to be honest enough to admit this, but for the sake of TRUTH I am. What's my truth? I needed to be loved and adored by others so much that I always felt the need to be great at something or attach myself to a group of people who would be worshipped by others.

I know at times it can be difficult to be completely honest with ourselves. We find ways to justify non-sense instead of facing the facts and accepting the TRUTH. Here's the danger in not being honest with ourselves. If we continue living this facade for too long, it can prolong our true greatness and our true happiness.

Daily Assignment:

- Write your Daily Affirmation on **My Powerful Affirmation's** pages in the back.
- Write down one thing you are grateful for and place in your **My Gratitude Jar.**

WEEK 3-DAY 2

BODY-(The TRUTH SHALL SET YOU FREE)

The media today has convinced us that if our bodies don't look the status quo of what they deem beautiful, then we should think less of ourselves. It's gotten so bad that people are enhancing parts of their body, taking drugs that guarantees weight loss, and even committing suicide because they view themselves as ugly. In most cases, the body that we currently have is the body that we created. The good news is that in most instances we can work to change our body once we decide to do so.

Answer the following question TRUTHFULLY.

On a scale of 1 to 10 how happy are you with the look and feel of your body? If you could change one thing about your body, what would it be and why?

_____

_____

_____

_____

_____

_____

Justin A. Davis

*What does God say about your BODY?

I Corinthians 6:19-20-Do you not know that your bodies are temples of the Holy Spirit, who is in you, whom you have received from God? (NIV Translation)

What is the 1 thing you need to change today to glorify God with your Body? How can you hold yourself accountable to this change?

_____

_____

_____

_____

_____

_____

_____

_____

_____

_____

_____

_____

Daily Assignment:

- Write your Daily Affirmation on **My Powerful Affirmation's** pages in the back.
- Write down one thing you are grateful for and place in your **My Gratitude Jar.**

WEEK 3- DAY 3

(BOND-THE TRUTH SHALL SET YOU FREE)

Social media has been a gift and a curse. It has allowed us to connect with people all over the world and see their life in ways that we have never been able to see before. The curse is that we have created relationships at a distance, yet we are trying to treat them as intimate relationships. Relationships are the most valuable resource on the planet. Trying to distinguish between who is a friend versus who is an acquaintance has become a challenge.

Answer the following question TRUTHFULLY.

What are the 3 most important qualities someone must have in order for you to consider them a friend? If you have no criteria, create 3 now.

_____

_____

_____

_____

_____

_____

_____

_____

_____

Justin A. Davis

*What does God say about BOND?

Proverbs 13:20-Walk with the wise and become wise, for a companion of fools suffers harm. (NIV Translation)

Who are the relationships if any, in your life currently that are causing you harm spiritually, physically, emotionally, or financially? Are you willing to end this relationship for the sake of your own growth? Explain your answer.

_____

_____

_____

_____

_____

_____

_____

_____

_____

_____

_____

Daily Assignment:

- Write your Daily Affirmation on **My Powerful Affirmation's** pages in the back.
- Write down one thing you are grateful for and place in your **My Gratitude Jar.**

WEEK 3-DAY 4

(BUSINESS-The TRUTH SHALL SET YOU FREE)

Our business or occupations are a huge part of our lives. As adults, most of us spend more time working than we do sleeping. The world can get so hectic and we can get so wrapped up in wanting more, that it can be difficult to have a good work-life balance. Some of us have been told that in order to have a happy life, we alone must be able to provide the finer things in life for our loved ones. The idea is cool, but is it practical for all? Sometimes it might be better to find balance between business and home if you want joy and peace.

Answer the following question TRUTHFULLY.

On a scale of 1 to 10 how happy are you with your work-life balance? Who is being impacted negatively the most by you being imbalanced in this area? How are they being impacted personally?

_____

_____

_____

_____

Justin A. Davis

*What does God say about BUSINESS (Occupation)?

Hebrews 13:5-Keep your lives free from love of money, and be content with what you have, because God has said. Never will I leave you; never will I forsake you." (NIV Translation)

What minor adjustment can you make today to show the person who is being negatively impacted by your work life imbalance, that you love them dearly?

_____

_____

_____

_____

_____

_____

_____

Daily Assignment:

- Write your Daily Affirmation on **My Powerful Affirmation's** pages in the back.
- Write down one thing you are grateful for and place in your **My Gratitude Jar.**

WEEK 3-DAY 5

BUDGET-(The TRUTH SHALL SET YOU FREE)

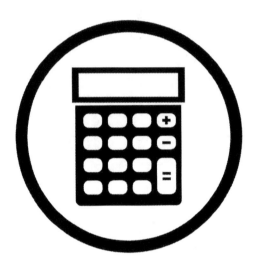

I need more clothes. I need more shoes. I need a nicer car. I need a bigger house. I need to go on a vacation. These are all thoughts that seem to come to our minds all the time. What is it about us wanting more all the time? Not only do we want more, that's not the real problem. Our real problem is that we want more now, and I mean like right now. So, when we want more now, what do most of us do? We find a way to get it. This type of mentality prevents us from making wise decisions with our money.

Answer the following question TRUTHFULLY.

How much money do you have in an emergency fund currently and how long did it take you to save it? If you don't have 3 to 6 months of your current expenses saved, how long will it take you to save this much?

_____

_____

_____

_____

_____

_____

_____

Justin A. Davis

*What does God say about BUDGET?

Proverbs 21:5-The plans of the diligent lead to profit as surely as haste leads to poverty. (NIV Translation)

What if anything, has prevented you from fully committing to a budget that will allow you to have 3 to 6 months of your expenses in an emergency fund? If you were fired today what would happen in your life for the people you love without this emergency fund?

_____

_____

_____

_____

_____

_____

_____

_____

_____

Daily Assignment:

- Write your Daily Affirmation on **My Powerful Affirmation's** pages in the back.
- Write down one thing you are grateful for and place in your **My Gratitude Jar.**

WEEK 3-DAY 6

BRAIN-(THE TRUTH SHALL SET YOU FREE)

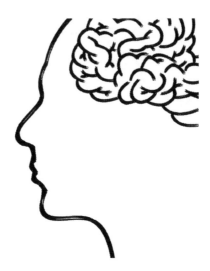

Our brains are the most powerful tools in the universe. They have used it to create cars, planes, bridges, underground tunnels, and the internet. We've even used it to figure out a way to send people into outer space. There is nothing that our brains can't accomplish. Since we have all been given this tool and we know its value, what are we doing to keep this tool in good working condition? The brain is like a sponge and it will absorb everything it is exposed to. Are we really treating our brain with as much value as we should?

Answer the following question TRUTHFULLY.

What daily exercises do you do as it relates to your brain? What do you do daily for the enrichment of your brain?

_____

_____

_____

_____

_____

_____

_____

Justin A. Davis

*What does God say about our BRAIN?

Romans 12:2-Do not conform to the pattern of this world, but be transformed by the renewing of your mind. Then you will be able to test and approve what God's will is—his good, pleasing and perfect will. (NIV Translation)

What are you doing, or can you do daily to renew your mind? What practice do you have in place or can you put in place to protect your mind from negative thoughts?

_____

_____

_____

_____

_____

_____

_____

_____

_____

Daily Assignment:

- Write your Daily Affirmation on **My Powerful Affirmation's** pages in the back.
- Write down one thing you are grateful for and place in your **My Gratitude Jar.**

Day 7 Reflecting on My Truth

For the last 6 days you have written down daily affirmations.

For this next exercise, I want you to go through your affirmations and rate them on a scale of 1 to 3.

<u>Rate Number</u>

1 = Living in My Truth
2 = Kind of Living in My Truth
3 = Currently not living in my Truth.

E. Choose an affirmation that is currently closest to your **TRUTH**. Give an example of how you are living that truth.

_____

_____

_____

_____

_____

_____

_____

_____

F. Choose an affirmation that is currently furthest from your **TRUTH.** Give an example of how you will take steps into making that your **TRUTH.**

_____

_____

_____

_____

_____

_____

_____

Justin A. Davis

WEEK 4

The TRUTH ABOUT THE ARMOR OF GOD

Ephesians 6 10-13 (NIV Translation)

[10] Finally, be strong in the Lord and in his mighty power. [11] Put on the full armor of God, so that you can take your stand against the devil's schemes. [12] For our struggle is not against flesh and blood, but against the rulers, against the authorities, against the powers of this dark world and against the spiritual forces of evil in the heavenly realms.[13] Therefore put on the full armor of God, so that when the day of evil comes, you may be able to stand your ground, and after you have done everything, to stand.

It's really hard to be strong as the scripture above says, when you feel so weak. So many of us are constantly looking for something that will give us the strength we feel we need. So many of us turn to our family or friends hoping that we can somehow find strength in them or at least feel supported. Regrettably, the thing we all find out sooner or later is that we can't find our strength in other people. The TRUTH is the only place we truly find strength for ourselves is by putting on the armor of God. If we take the steps that God tells us to take as it relates to putting on his armor, the strength that we seek will not only be supplied, but we will also be able to live in victory.

Daily Assignment:

- Write your Daily Affirmation on **My Powerful Affirmation's** pages in the back.
- Write down one thing you are grateful for and place in your **My Gratitude Jar.**

WEEK 4-DAY 2

(TRUTH ABOUT THE ARMOR OF GOD –
TRUTH AND RIGHTEOUSNESS)

Telling the truth and doing the right thing is something that seems to be going out of style today? For some reason, we've gotten to the point that we believe that we can be dishonest and still expect life to give us the desires of our heart. Sure, it might seem like there are people in life that are getting by with being deceitful, but when you pull the covers back from their life, they are miserable most of the time. Being pure in heart will usually give us the best chance at happiness and peace.

Answer the following question TRUTHFULLY.

What is one thing you need to be truthful about with yourself or with a loved one that you've been unwilling to acknowledge?

_____

_____

_____

_____

_____

_____

_____

Justin A. Davis

*What does God say about TRUTH AND RIGHTEOUSNESS?

Ephesians-4:15 Instead, speaking the truth in love, we will grow to become in every respect the mature body of him who is the head, that is, Christ. (NIV Translation)

Acknowledge 1 more Truth that you need to admit to yourself or a loved one. How will this help to improve your life for the better?

_____

_____

_____

_____

_____

_____

_____

_____

_____

_____

_____

Daily Assignment:

- Write your Daily Affirmation on **My Powerful Affirmation's** pages in the back.
- Write down one thing you are grateful for and place in your **My Gratitude Jar.**

WEEK 4-DAY 3

(TRUTH ABOUT THE ARMOR OF GOD-GOSPEL OF PEACE)

If you've lived life long enough, then you have come to know the importance of having peace. As we get older there are so many more responsibilities that we have, that make it difficult to truly relax. Going to work, doing the chores around the house, being a good parent, and trying to be a good spouse pulls us in so many different directions. Finding peace in our life is the most important thing, that we all need. We should always aim to bring peace and be at peace as often as we can.

Answer the following question TRUTHFULLY.

What is the one area of your life that needs the most peace? What is the major obstacle that is preventing this peace?

_____

_____

_____

_____

_____

_____

_____

_____

_____

Justin A. Davis

*What does God say about PEACE?

Matthew 5:9-Blessed are the peacemakers, for they will be called children of God. (NIV Translation)

Spend some time thinking about the obstacle that is preventing peace in your life. Choose one behavior you can change, that will bring you more Peace.

_____

_____

_____

_____

_____

_____

_____

_____

_____

_____

Daily Assignment:

- Write your Daily Affirmation on **My Powerful Affirmation's** pages in the back.
- Write down one thing you are grateful for and place in your **My Gratitude Jar.**

WEEK 4-DAY 4

(TRUTH ABOUT THE ARMOR OF GOD-FAITH)

Faith is the substance of things hoped for in the evidence of things not seen. Most Christians know this bible verse and throw it around so casually that you would think they are living a life full of faith. The reality is, most Christians lack faith. There are levels to faith. What one person can believe God for is completely different than what someone else might be capable of believing. The truth about faith though, is that whatever level of faith we currently have, there is another level higher than that.

Answer the following question TRUTHFULLY.

What is one area of your life that needs a greater level of faith so that you can truly have what you want?

_____

_____

_____

_____

_____

_____

_____

_____

Justin A. Davis

*What does God say about FAITH?

Matthew 17:20-He replied, "Because you have so little faith. Truly I tell you, if you have faith as small as a mustard seed, you can say to this mountain, "Move from here to there," and it will move. Nothing will be impossible for you".

(NIV Translation)

Speak life to whatever situation or area of your life that needs more Faith by writing it down and speaking to it. Read this statement out loud. "I may only have a little bit of Faith, but God said that's all I need." You will conform to my will with God's help!"

_____

_____

_____

_____

_____

_____

_____

_____

_____

_____

Daily Assignment:

- Write your Daily Affirmation on **My Powerful Affirmation's** pages in the back.
- Write down one thing you are grateful for and place in your **My Gratitude Jar.**

WEEK 4- DAY 5

(TRUTH ABOUT THE ARMOR OF GOD-SALVATION)

As believers, we are told that Jesus went to prepare a place for us so that when we are no longer able to be in our bodies, we have a place with him and God. This is the idea of salvation that many of us hold on to for our entire lives. If many of us were truthful with ourselves, we would have to admit that our salvation is tied fear. If I don't do what God tells me, I might not make it to heaven. This idea of salvation will only take us so far. If we are worshipping God out of fear, salvation might be the least of our worries.

Answer the following question TRUTHFULLY.

If God were to ask you right now, why do you think you should go to heaven, what would you say?

_____

_____

_____

_____

_____

_____

_____

Justin A. Davis

*What does God say about SALVATION?

Titus 3:5-He saved us, not because of the righteous things we had done, but because of his mercy. He saved us through the washing of rebirth and renewal by the Holy Spirit. (NIV Translation)

Thank God for your relationship with him. Not just because you believe you will see him one day in heaven, but because he has shown himself to you while on earth. Write a note to God, specifically stating how he has shown himself to you.

_____

_____

_____

_____

_____

_____

_____

_____

_____

<u>Daily Assignment:</u>

- Write your Daily Affirmation on **My Powerful Affirmation's** pages in the back.
- Write down one thing you are grateful for and place in your **My Gratitude Jar.**

WEEK 4-DAY 6

(TRUTH ABOUT THE ARMOR OF GOD-WORD OF GOD)

The bible is by far the most influential book of all-time. Not only has it been the foundation of some countries plans of government, but it has also outsold any other book in history by an unbelievable margin. This alone should tell us how powerful God's Word really is. People have laid down their very life in defense of God's Word. God's Word is so life changing that when you begin to really understand and apply the fullness of his teachings, there is nothing on the face of the earth that is not available to us.

Answer the following question TRUTHFULLY.

On a scale of 1-10 how well versed are you in the God's principles not just the stories of the Word of God? What 3 principles of the Word of God are at the forefront of your life?

_____

_____

_____

_____

_____

_____

_____

*What does God say about his WORD?

Matthew 4:4-Jesus answered, "It is written: "Man shall not live on bread alone, but on every word that comes from the mouth of God"." (NIV Translation)

How can you use God's Word, to better yourself and better the people that God has placed in your life?

_____

_____

_____

_____

_____

_____

_____

_____

_____

Daily Assignment:

- Write your Daily Affirmation on **My Powerful Affirmation's** pages in the back.
- Write down one thing you are grateful for and place in your **My Gratitude Jar.**

Day 7 Reflecting on My Truth

For the last 6 days you have written down daily affirmations.

For this next exercise, I want you to go through your affirmations and rate them on a scale of 1 to 3.

<u>Rate Number</u>

1 = Living in My Truth
2 = Kind of Living in My Truth
3 = Currently not living in my Truth.

G. Choose an affirmation that is currently your closest to your **TRUTH**. Give an example of how you are living that truth.

_____

_____

_____

_____

_____

_____

_____

_____

H. Choose an affirmation that is currently furthest from your **TRUTH**. Give an example of how you will take steps into making that your **TRUTH.**

_____

_____

_____

_____

_____

_____

_____

_____

_____

Justin A. Davis

WEEK 5

God's Truth leads to Protection

Isiah 41:10 (NIV Translation)

So do not fear, for I am with you;
do not be dismayed, for I am your God.
I will strengthen you and help you;
I will uphold you with my righteous right hand.

There is an old saying, "God protects fools and babies". Let's just say that God protected me and leave it at that. There were so many instances God protected me when I was living a life that I knew wasn't right. The TRUTH is, he protected me when I found myself in brawls at fraternity fights that could have ended in somebody being dead or at least seriously injured. He protected me in my late teens and early twenties when I partied too hard and was stupid enough to drive home drunk afterwards. Most importantly, he protected me by keeping me in my right mind when my wife lost her job, she was diagnosed with breast-cancer, my mother died, our premature twins died all within a 10-month period. The great thing about God's protection is that it not only protects us, but he will protect the people and things closest to us. God's protection is one of the most important things in life that he offers us. We'd be a fool not to take him up on it. If you haven't tried it yet, I'm here to tell you that it will get you through some of my darkest hours.

Daily Assignment:

- Write your Daily Affirmation on **My Powerful Affirmation's** pages in the back.
- Write down one thing you are grateful for and place in your **My Gratitude Jar.**

WEEK 5-DAY 2

(GOD'S TRUTH LEADS TO PROTECTING YOU)

God is such a huge God that at times we can feel unworthy of approaching him for what we need. The crazy thing though, is that God knows when we feel like that. He created us, so he is always in tune with what we are thinking, how we are feeling, and why we are doing what we are doing. Sometimes, we might not even know. So, because of this, even when we can't protect ourselves, God is always on the job.

Answer the following question TRUTHFULLY.

Explain a time that it was only through God's grace and protection, that your life was saved or something terrible didn't happen to you?

_____

_____

_____

_____

_____

_____

_____

_____

Justin A. Davis

*What does God say about his PROTECTING YOU?

2 *Thessalonians 3:3-But the Lord is faithful, and he will strengthen you and protect you from the evil one. (NIV Translation)*

Write down 2 more times God protected you from harm, and thank him for watching over your life?

_____

_____

_____

_____

_____

_____

_____

_____

_____

_____

_____

<u>Daily Assignment:</u>

- Write your Daily Affirmation on **My Powerful Affirmation's** pages in the back.
- Write down one thing you are grateful for and place in your **My Gratitude Jar.**

WEEK 5-DAY 3

(GOD'S TRUTH LEADS TO PROTECTING YOUR FRIENDS)

Jesus came to earth for so many reasons. We all must agree that one of the most important reasons he came, is so we can learn how to model his life, and follow his teaching. The most important sacrifice that's ever been made was done by Jesus on the cross. He gave up his life so that mankind would be saved, and we would be able to have a closer relationship with God. We may not sacrifice our lives as Jesus did for us, but we can make sacrifices to protect each other whenever possible

Answer the following question TRUTHFULLY.

Explain a time in your life that you felt compelled to be a protector of a friend who was not able to protect themselves?

_____

_____

_____

_____

_____

*What does God say about him PROTECTING YOUR FRIENDS?

John 15:13-Greater love has no one than this, to lay down one's life for one's friends. (NIV Translation)

Write down 1 Friend in your life that you will be forever committed to protecting and explain why you chose that Friend.

_____

_____

_____

_____

_____

_____

_____

Daily Assignment:

- Write your Daily Affirmation on **My Powerful Affirmation's** pages in the back.
- Write down one thing you are grateful for and place in your **My Gratitude Jar.**

WEEK 5-DAY 4

(GOD'S TRUTH LEADS TO PROTECTING YOUR CHILDREN)

The world we live in can be very scary. With everyone having so much access to the internet there seems to be no limit to what our children can be exposed to. From extreme hatred, to bullying, to pedophiles, our children can be introduced to things, that we as parents have very little control over. We must trust that even in this world, God is in complete control and he will do what he has always done in protecting those who can't protect themselves.

Answer the following question TRUTHFULLY.

What is one thing that your parent or guardian taught you that has protected you from danger as an adult?

_____

_____

_____

_____

_____

_____

Justin A. Davis

*What does God say about him PROTECTING YOUR CHILDREN?

Proverbs 22:6-Start children off on the way they should go, and even when they are old whey will not turn from it. (NIV Translation)

What will be the one thing you teach a child, to ensure they have the knowledge to live their best life as an adult?

_____

_____

_____

_____

_____

_____

_____

_____

_____

Daily Assignment:

- Write your Daily Affirmation on **My Powerful Affirmation's** pages in the back.
- Write down one thing you are grateful for and place in your **My Gratitude Jar.**

WEEK 5-DAY 5

(GOD'S TRUTH LEADS TO PROTECTING YOUR MARRIAGE/RELATIONSHIP)

Most little girls dream about their prince, and one day being married. They dream of wearing the white dress, walking down the aisle, getting the ring and saying, "I Do!" But before they say "I Do!" the minister in most instances speaks about how she and her husband can protect their marriage. Many people don't realize how important this conversation before the "I Do's, really is. The things that are spoken are the bedrock of a strong marriage.

Answer the following question TRUTHFULY.

Married or not, what is the most important characteristic for you in a significant other as it relates to how you want to be treated?

_____

_____

_____

_____

_____

_____

Justin A. Davis

*What does God say about him PROTECTING YOUR RELATIONSHIP?

Colossians 3:18-19-Wives, submit to your husbands, as is fitting in the Lord. Husbands, love your wives, and do not be harsh with them. (NIV Translation)

If you are, or plan to be a husband or wife, do you or will you have a difficult time following God's commandment to love or submit, if your partner does not? Why is it or would it be such a difficult thing to do?

_____
_____
_____
_____
_____
_____
_____
_____
_____
_____
_____

Daily Assignment:

- Write your Daily Affirmation on **My Powerful Affirmation's** pages in the back.
- Write down one thing you are grateful for and place in your **My Gratitude Jar.**

WEEK 5-DAY 6

(GOD'S TRUTH LEADS TO PROTECTING YOUR HOME)

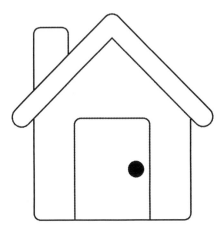

There are basic needs that we all need as human beings. We all need food and water to survive. We need clothing, so we can protect ourselves from the changing weather. We all need shelter to protect us from the environment. These are basic needs but there is something that we all need as well. To feel connected as a person, we need a HOME. Those who have ever gone without it fully understand what I mean. Living in a shelter is very different from having a home. A home allows for joy, love, and peace for all who are present.

Answer the following question TRUTHFULLY.

Is your current home a place that is conducive for love, joy, and peace for all who live or visit you? Explain your answer.

_____

_____

_____

_____

_____

_____

_____

Justin A. Davis

*What does God say about him PROTECTING YOUR HOME?

Isaiah 32:18-My people will abide in peaceful dwelling places, in secure homes, in undisturbed places of rest. (NIV Translation)

It is God's desire that we live in homes that are peaceful, secure, and in quiet resting places. Are there any issues that prevent this from being the case in your current home? What are you willing to do about it?

_____

_____

_____

_____

_____

_____

_____

_____

_____

_____

_____

Daily Assignment:

- Write your Daily Affirmation on **My Powerful Affirmation's** pages in the back.
- Write down one thing you are grateful for and place in your **My Gratitude Jar.**

Day 7 Reflecting on My Truth

For the last 6 days you have written down daily affirmations.

For this next exercise, I want you to go through your affirmations and rate them on a scale of 1 to 3.

Rate Number

1 = Living in My Truth
2 = Kind of Living in My Truth
3 = Currently not living in my Truth.

I. Choose an affirmation that is currently closest to your **TRUTH**. Give an example of how you are living that truth.

_____

_____

_____

_____

_____

_____

_____

J. Choose an affirmation that is currently furthest from your **TRUTH**. Give an example of how you will take steps into making that your **TRUTH.**

_____

_____

_____

_____

_____

_____

_____

Justin A. Davis

WEEK 6

God's Truth Leads to Wisdom

— Proverbs 4:6-7a (NIV Translation)

Do not forsake wisdom, and she will protect you; lover her, and she will watch over you. The beginning of wisdom is this: get wisdom.

Accepting the word of God was the best decision of my life. I gained so much wisdom about the world and myself once I did. It was as if my mind was open to receive so much and I started soaking it all in.

True Wisdom is living life according to God's plan. If you think about it, it makes sense. God's plan is the best plan for you. You will be "Living Your Blessed Life". Now, of course, just because you make wise choices, doesn't mean you're protected from bad things happening to you. Sometimes, someone else' choices may affect you, and you have to live with those consequences. But when you live a "wise" life, you're protected from the negative consequences of your bad choices.

Here are 3 things you can do to gain wisdom:

1. Rely on God
2. Think Before you Act
3. Use Failure as a Teacher

Daily Assignment:

- Write your Daily Affirmation on **My Powerful Affirmation's** pages in the back.
- Write down one thing you are grateful for and place in your **My Gratitude Jar.**

63

WEEK 6-DAY 2

(GOD'S TRUTH LEADS TO WISDOM IN YOUR PERSONAL LIFE)

Being an adult can be difficult at times. There are so many things that we are responsible for, so many people that are depending on us, and so many tasks that we need to handle, that it can be overwhelming trying to figure out what to prioritize. We must make choices and of course those choices will have consequences good or bad. So, it's important to have a certain level of wisdom when making decisions that will not only impact your life but the people you care about as well.

Answer the following question TRUTHFULLY.

On a scale of 1-10 what is your personal track record in using wisdom when making decisions for your life? Give 2 examples to support your decision.

_____

_____

_____

_____

_____

_____

Justin A. Davis

*What does God say about WISDOM in your PERSONAL LIFE?

James 1:5- *If any of you lacks wisdom, you should ask God, who gives generously to all without finding fault, and it will be given to you.*
(NIV Translation)

Wisdom is a gift from God that is available to us all and is something that we could use a bit more of. Choose one area in your life right now and write down a prayer asking God for more wisdom. Tell him why you want it?

_____

_____

_____

_____

_____

_____

_____

_____

_____

_____

Daily Assignment:

- Write your Daily Affirmation on **My Powerful Affirmation's** pages in the back.
- Write down one thing you are grateful for and place in your **My Gratitude Jar.**

WEEK 6-DAY 3

(GOD'S TRUTH LEADS TO WISDOM IN YOUR FINANCES)

Bankruptcy, Pay Day loans, foreclosures, repossessions, liens, the list can go on forever. If these are things that you have experienced or are currently experiencing, you know how difficult this can be to endure. Yet, in most cases if we are honest with ourselves, we could have made different choices financially to prevent this from happening. Financial wisdom is something that we could all use a bit more information about, but we must be willing to act on the information once it is given.

Answer the following question TRUTHFULLY.

Name 1 habit you know you need to break that is contributing to your finances negatively. Why haven't you broken this habit yet?

_____

_____

_____

_____

_____

_____

Justin A. Davis

*What does God say about WISDOM in FINANCES?

Proverbs 21:5-The plans of the diligent lead to profit as surely as haste leads to poverty." (NIV Translation)

Do you consider yourself a diligent person or a person of haste financially? If so, give an example? What actions will you take to be more diligent financially?

_____

_____

_____

_____

_____

_____

_____

_____

_____

_____

Daily Assignment:

- Write your Daily Affirmation on **My Powerful Affirmation's** pages in the back.
- Write down one thing you are grateful for and place in your **My Gratitude Jar.**

WEEK 6-DAY 4

(GOD'S TRUTH LEADS TO WISDOM IN YOUR SPEECH)

We've all heard the saying, "Sticks and stones can break my bones, but words can never hurt me". This is one of the lies that we are told as a child that has led to tremendous hurt and pain over the years. Not only can words hurt others, but they can hurt us as well if we don't use wisdom in our speech. Life and death are in the power of the tongue and when we choose to speak foolishly, death is usually the outcome.

Answer the following question TRUTHFULLY.

Write down 2 incidents in your life where your foolish choice of words led to detrimental situations for you or a loved one?

_____

_____

_____

_____

_____

_____

_____

Justin A. Davis

*What does God say about WISDOM in SPEECH?

Luke 21:15-For I will give you words and wisdom that none of your adversaries will be able to resist or contradict. (NIV Translation)

Write down 3 things that you promise to never allow yourself to repeat to a person you care about.

_____

_____

_____

_____

_____

_____

_____

_____

_____

_____

Daily Assignment:

- Write your Daily Affirmation on **My Powerful Affirmation's** pages in the back.
- Write down one thing you are grateful for and place in your **My Gratitude Jar.**

WEEK 6-DAY 5

(GOD'S TRUTH LEADS TO WISDOM IN YOUR CHOICES)

"Choosy moms choose Jiff". I'm not sure if you remember that peanut butter commercial or not, but if you don't it was popular in the 80's and 90's. The crazy thing is that a woman tried to sue the company saying she looked like a bad mother if she didn't give her child Jiff. The responsibility of our choices rests solely on us. We must be responsible for our actions and stop pointing the blame at others.

Answer the following question TRUTHFULLY.

If you could have a do over in life, what is one choice that you would make differently? How would that have changed the course of your life?

_____

_____

_____

_____

_____

_____

*What does God say about WISDOM in our CHOICES?

Ephesians 5:15-16-Be very careful, then, how you live—not as unwise but as wise, making the most of every opportunity……. (NIV Translation)

Write down the 3 things that occupies most of your down time. Is this the most effective way to use your time? Why or Why not?

_____

_____

_____

_____

_____

_____

_____

_____

_____

_____

_____

Daily Assignment:

- Write your Daily Affirmation on **My Powerful Affirmation's** pages in the back.
- Write down one thing you are grateful for and place in your **My Gratitude Jar.**

WEEK 6-DAY 6

(GOD'S TRUTH LEADS TO WISDOM IN YOUR RELATIONSHIPS)

There have been studies done on the importance of relationships. Babies who were isolated from any human contact for the first weeks of their lives have died due to lack of contact. As humans we need interaction with each other. That could be a gift, but it can also be a curse if we choose to interact with the wrong people at the wrong time. Our relationships will usually dictate the type of life we will have. It's our job to choose them wisely.

Answer the following question TRUTHFULLY.

Of all the intimate relationships you currently have, which 1 relationship is the greatest stressor in your life? How is the relationship hurting you?

_____

_____

_____

_____

_____

_____

_____

Justin A. Davis

*What does God say about WISDOM in our RELATIONSHIPS?

2 Corinthians 6:14-Do not be yoked together with unbelievers. For what do righteousness and wickedness have in common? Or what fellowship can light have with darkness? (NIV Translation)

What practical steps can you put in your life to build boundaries for yourself as it relates to shielding yourself from relationships that are harmful to you?

_____

_____

_____

_____

_____

_____

_____

_____

_____

_____

_____

<u>Daily Assignment:</u>

- Write your Daily Affirmation on **My Powerful Affirmation's** pages in the back.
- Write down one thing you are grateful for and place in your **My Gratitude Jar.**

Day 7 Reflecting on My Truth

For the last 6 days you have written down daily affirmations.

For this next exercise, I want you to go through your affirmations and rate them on a scale of 1 to 3.

<u>Rate Number</u>

1 = Living in My Truth
2 = Kind of Living in My Truth
3 = Currently not living in my Truth.

K. Choose an affirmation that is currently closest to your **TRUTH**. Give an example of how you are living that truth.

_____

_____

_____

_____

_____

_____

_____

L. Choose an affirmation that is currently furthest from your **TRUTH.** Give an example of how you will take steps into making that your **TRUTH.**

_____

_____

_____

_____

_____

_____

_____

_____

Justin A. Davis

WEEK 7

God's Truth Leads to Prosperity

Mathew 6:31-34 (NIV Translation)

³¹ So do not worry, saying, 'What shall we eat?' or 'What shall we drink?' or 'What shall we wear?' ³² For the pagans run after all these things, and your heavenly Father knows that you need them. ³³ But seek first his kingdom and his righteousness, and all these things will be given to you as well. ³⁴ Therefore do not worry about tomorrow, for tomorrow will worry about itself. Each day has enough trouble of its own.

When pastor's throw these scriptures around in the pulpit, you usually see all the Saints nodding their heads in agreement. You hear a lot of Amens and a lot of Touch-your-neighbor sayings about how God will provide. If we want to put the TRUTH on the table though, most believers don't know how to live out this scripture. I see so many people stressing about money. It breaks up families. It causes people to lose their homes. I've even seen people die over the stress of money problems. Worrying about money is a sign of lack of faith in God in that particular area of your life. Trust that God will provide, and he will.

Daily Assignment:

- Write your Daily Affirmation on **My Powerful Affirmation's** pages in the back.
- Write down one thing you are grateful for and place in your **My Gratitude Jar.**

WEEK 7-DAY 2

(GOD'S TRUTH LEADS TO PROSPERITY IN YOUR PERSONAL LIFE)

Why does it seem like some people have all the luck while others can't seem to catch a break? No matter what country you travel to, what field of endeavor you analyze, or what economic system you study, there will always seem to be individuals who seem to prosper while others suffer. I'm not saying it's right, but to ignore it would be a lie. If even 1 person can prosper, there must be a way for everyone on earth to find prosperity.

Answer the following question TRUTHFULLY.

Do you believe you deserve prosperity? Explain your answer by giving 2 examples of actions that you execute in your life that align you with prosperity.

_____

_____

_____

_____

_____

_____

Justin A. Davis

*What does God say about PROSPERITY in your PERSONAL LIFE?

Philippians 4:19-And my God will meet all your needs according to the riches of glory in Christ Jesus (NIV Translation)

Write down at least one action that you are willing to begin implementing in your life that aligns with prosperity principles?

_____

_____

_____

_____

_____

_____

_____

_____

_____

_____

_____

<u>Daily Assignment:</u>

- Write your Daily Affirmation on **My Powerful Affirmation's** pages in the back.
- Write down one thing you are grateful for and place in your **My Gratitude Jar.**

WEEK 7-DAY 3

(GOD'S TRUTH LEADS TO PROSPERITY IN YOUR FAMILY)

Have you ever thought about the fact that most of the wealth in the world is held by a small percentage of people? Really take a step back and think about that for a moment. How is it that 1% of the population owns almost 50% of the world's wealth? There must be a hidden truth that these people know that the rest of us don't. If not, then that would mean that God is not a just God and we know that isn't the case.

Answer the following question TRUTHFULLY.

What have you done to secure you and your family's financial future? If you haven't done anything, what has stopped you?

_____

_____

_____

_____

_____

*What does God say about PROSPERITY in our LINEAGE?

Deuteronomy 8:18- But remember the Lord your God, for it is he who gives you the ability to produce wealth, and so confirms his covenant, which he swore to your ancestors, as it is today. (NIV Translations)

What change in your household finances can you make right now, to ensure that you are taking a step toward financial security?

_____

_____

_____

_____

_____

_____

_____

Daily Assignment:

- Write your Daily Affirmation on **My Powerful Affirmation's** pages in the back.
- Write down one thing you are grateful for and place in your **My Gratitude Jar.**

WEEK 7-DAY 4

(GOD'S TRUTH LEADS TO PROSPERITY IN YOUR BODY)

With social media, the internet, plastic surgery, and all other sorts of industries that convince people that their body needs to look a certain way to be acceptable, it's hard for most people to think about anything else accept their physical image. While exercising is important, there are numerous other things that we must do to make sure we are taking care of ourselves now and in the future.

Answer the following question TRUTHFULLY.

On a scale of 1 to 10 how would you rank yourself regarding taking care of your spiritual and mental health? Give 2 examples to support your answer.

_____

_____

_____

_____

_____

_____

_____

_____

Justin A. Davis

*What does God say about PROSPERITY in your BODY?

1 Timothy 4:8- For physical training is of some value, but godliness has value for all things, holding promise for both the present life and the life to come. (NIV Translation)

Write down 2 activities you can implement immediately so that you can improve your spiritual and mental health.

_____

_____

_____

_____

_____

_____

_____

_____

Daily Assignment:

- Write your Daily Affirmation on **My Powerful Affirmation's** pages in the back.
- Write down one thing you are grateful for and place in your **My Gratitude Jar.**

WEEK 7-DAY 5

(GOD'S TRUTH LEADS TO PROSPERITY IN YOUR RELATIONSHIPS)

Relationships can be complicated. Trying to figure out how to treat someone while trying to figure out what you will allow from them regarding how they treat you, is a challenging task. We are constantly changing and growing individually, which not only puts strain on us, but even more of a strain on the relationships we have. There is power in finding balance in your relationships.

Answer the following question TRUTHFULLY.

Is prospering in your intimate relationships just as important as prospering financially in your life? Give 2 examples in your life to support your answer.

_____

_____

_____

_____

_____

_____

_____

_____

_____

Justin A. Davis

*What does God say about PROSPERITY in your RELATIONSHIPS?

1 Corinthians 13:4-8- Love is patient and kind; love does not envy or boast; it is not proud. It does not dishonor others; it is not self-seeking, it is not easily angered, it keeps no record of wrongs. Love does not delight in evil but rejoices with the truth. (NIV Translation)

Acknowledge 1 relationship in your life currently that you would like to see more prosperity in. Write down 1 thing you are willing to do tomorrow to see this prosperity manifest.

_____

_____

_____

_____

_____

_____

_____

_____

_____

_____

_____

Daily Assignment:

- Write your Daily Affirmation on **My Powerful Affirmation's** pages in the back.
- Write down one thing you are grateful for and place in your **My Gratitude Jar.**

WEEK 7-DAY 6

(GOD'S TRUTH LEADS TO PROSPERITY IN YOUR CAREER)

Working a 9 to 5 is something that most people have to do in order to support their families. Some people find themselves in jobs that they don't like just to make ends meet. They are not living in their TRUTH or using their God given talents. When we find ourselves in this position it's easy to complain and give a terrible effort because we aren't' happy with our situation. The mature thing to do, is work to our fullest potential and pray that God will honor our prayers for better circumstances.

Answer the following question TRUTHFULLY.

On a scale of 1 to 10 what type of effort do you put in on your job when you know nobody is watching. Based on your score, are you happy with yourself? Explain your answer.

_____

_____

_____

_____

_____

_____

_____

_____

_____

*What does God say about PROSPERITY in your CAREER?

Proverbs 10:4- Lazy hands make for poverty, but diligent hands bring wealth. (NIV Translation)

Write down what you want God to do for you concerning your next career promotion and begin praying every night for God to help you accomplish it.

_____

_____

_____

_____

_____

_____

_____

_____

_____

_____

<u>Daily Assignment:</u>

- Write your Daily Affirmation on **My Powerful Affirmation's** pages in the back.
- Write down one thing you are grateful for and place in your **My Gratitude Jar.**

Day 7 Reflecting on My Truth

For the last 6 days you have written down daily affirmations.

For this next exercise, I want you to go through your affirmations and rate them on a scale of 1 to 3.

Rate Number

1 = Living in My Truth
2 = Kind of Living in My Truth
3 = Currently not living in my Truth.

M. Choose an affirmation that is currently closest to your **TRUTH**. Give an example of how you are living that truth.

_____

_____

_____

_____

_____

_____

_____

_____

N. Choose an affirmation that is currently furthest from your **TRUTH**. Give an example of how you will take steps into making that your **TRUTH.**

_____

_____

_____

_____

_____

_____

_____

_____

WEEK 8

God's Truth Leads to Restoration

Jeremiah 30 18-19 (NIV Translation)

18 "This is what the LORD says: "'I will restore the fortunes of Jacob's tents and have compassion on his dwellings; the city will be rebuilt on her ruins, and the palace will stand in its proper place.

19 From them will come songs of thanksgiving and the sound of rejoicing. I will add to their numbers, and they will not be decreased; I will bring them honor, and they will not be disdained.

There's a huge difference between replacing and restoring. There comes a time in everyone's life that restoration is all that we want. I can remember a time in life that I felt like I lost everything that mattered most to me. The crazy thing about it, is that I think it hurt so much because I never saw it coming. No matter what the incident was that happened to each of us, when things blindside us, restoration is needed. When we lose something that we hold dear, not matter what it is, our heart aches. Replacing is something we can do for ourselves and others. Restoration is something God has to do for each and every one of us.

<u>Daily Assignment:</u>

- Write your Daily Affirmation on **My Powerful Affirmation's** pages in the back.
- Write down one thing you are grateful for and place in your **My Gratitude Jar.**

WEEK 8-DAY 2

(GOD'S TRUTH LEADS TO RESTORATION OF YOUR MIND)

Our minds are the most amazing thing God has ever created. It's been said that at best, as human beings we use 10 percent of our brain's capacity. Think about how crazy that sounds. With all the things that we've been able to accomplish, we've only tapped into 10 percent. Think about the amount of information we have stored in our brains. That can be good and bad. Good because we can learn anything and everything. Bad because we can remember anything and everything. Sometimes those negative memories can cause emotional damage. We have to learn to Let Go and Let God. We have to lean on God for restoration of our mind.

Answer the following question TRUTHFULLY.

What's one incident that occurred in your life that you have yet to overcome? How has this created stress or dysfunction in your life currently?

_____

_____

_____

_____

_____

_____

*What does God say about RESTORATION OF YOUR MIND?

Philippians 4:6-7- Do not be anxious about anything, but in every situation by prayer and petition, with thanksgiving, present your request to God. And the peace of God, which transcends all understanding, will guard your hearts and your minds in Christ Jesus. (NIV Translation)

Write down a prayer that asks God to restore your mind by allowing you to release the negative thoughts associated with the incident you wrote down previously. Say this prayer consistently until God has restored your mind.

_____

_____

_____

_____

_____

_____

_____

_____

_____

_____

Daily Assignment:

- Write your Daily Affirmation on **My Powerful Affirmation's** pages in the back.
- Write down one thing you are grateful for and place in your **My Gratitude Jar.**

WEEK 8-DAY 3

(GOD'S TRUTH LEADS TO RESTORATION OF YOUR HEALTH)

Whether old age, poor diet, family genetics, or just lack of exercise, most people don't do the best job of keeping their bodies healthy. As we have gotten away from being hunters and gathers and have become a more stable society, we have begun to take our bodies for granted. With so many pharmaceutical drugs on the market we can now pop a pill for just about everything. The sad thing though is that our bodies are suffering more than we know. Today more than ever, we need our bodies restored.

Answer the following question TRUTHFULLY.

On a scale of 1-10 how physically healthy are you? If you are less than a 10 what can you do differently tomorrow to move towards the 10. If you are a 10, write out a thank you to God for helping you reach maximum health.

_____

_____

_____

_____

_____

_____

_____

_____

Justin A. Davis

*What does God say about RESTORATION OF YOUR HEALTH?

Jeremiah 30:17-"But I will restore you to health and heal your wounds," declares the Lord. (NIV Translation)

What area of your physical health is in most need of restoration? Write down a request from God to restore your health in this area and pray about it daily. If you are a 10 revisit your previous thank you and give him daily thanks moving forward.

_____

_____

_____

_____

_____

_____

_____

_____

_____

_____

_____

_____

Daily Assignment:

- Write your Daily Affirmation on **My Powerful Affirmation's** pages in the back.
- Write down one thing you are grateful for and place in your **My Gratitude Jar.**

WEEK 8-DAY 4

(GOD'S TRUTH LEADS TO RESTORATION OF YOUR SPIRIT)

At some point in most people's life, they will feel lost. I'm not talking about the type of lost like not knowing exactly where you are going. I'm talking about that type of lost like I don't know what's happening in my life right now. Life throws lots of challenges our way all the time, but sometimes it can just get overwhelming. Stressors like our children, spouses, careers, health problems, money problems, loss of a loved one lead us to needing restoration at some point. When you go through things like this you must look to something greater than yourself to reconnect yourself with your spirit.

Answer the following question TRUTHFULLY.

Is this a time in your life that you need restoration? If so, be honest with God about what really has you feeling lost and write it down. If not, think of a time in your life that you were and write down how you overcame it.

_____

_____

_____

_____

_____

_____

*What does God say about RESTORATION OF YOU?

1 Peter 5:10-And the God of all grace, who called you to his eternal glory in Christ, after you have suffered a little while, will himself restore you and make you strong, firm and steadfast. (NIV Translation)

Write down as many areas of your life as you can think of that needs to be restored.

_____

_____

_____

_____

_____

_____

_____

_____

_____

_____

_____

Daily Assignment:

- Write your Daily Affirmation on **My Powerful Affirmation's** pages in the back.
- Write down one thing you are grateful for and place in your **My Gratitude Jar.**

WEEK 8-DAY 5

(GOD'S TRUTH LEADS TO RESTORATION OF YOUR FORTUNE)

There has been story after story about people who have lost their fortunes. Sometimes it's due to riotous living and others it's due to unforeseen circumstances. But whenever and however it happens, it is devastating. If you have ever gone through a situation that left you wondering if there really is a God, then you know what I mean. Losing your wealth, your family, your health, and your fortune is a difficult thing to overcome. But, there is something that you can turn to even in a situation like this. Turn to God.

Answer the following question TRUTHFULLY.

Write down 2 incidents in your life that you questioned God's existence because so much loss and pain happened in your life so quickly. How did you overcome it?

_____

_____

_____

_____

_____

_____

_____

*What does God say about RESTORATION OF YOUR FORTUNE?

Job 42:10- After Job had prayed for his friends, the Lord restored his fortunes and gave him twice as much as he had before. (NIV Translation)

Of the things that you lost or the pain that you experienced during the incidents mentioned in the previous question, how many of those things has God restored in some way? Explain your answer.

_____

_____

_____

_____

_____

_____

_____

_____

_____

_____

Daily Assignment:

- Write your Daily Affirmation on **My Powerful Affirmation's** pages in the back.
- Write down one thing you are grateful for and place in your **My Gratitude Jar.**

WEEK 8-DAY 6

(GOD'S TRUTH LEADS TO RESTORATION OF YOUR RELATIONSHIP WITH GOD)

Most people can remember a time in their life that they've done something degrading or something they are not proud of. It's hard to go through life without getting into some crazy situations and making some decisions that we later regret. During those times, most of us are pretty hard on ourselves. Sometimes it even gets to the point where we are so ashamed, we believe God wants nothing else to do with us. God will never turn his back on us. It is us that moves away from him.

Answer the following question TRUTHFULLY.

What is the most shameful thing you have ever done to cause you to believe that you are not worthy of being in relationship with God? (This is for your eyes only.)

_____

_____

_____

_____

_____

_____

_____

Justin A. Davis

*What does God say about RESTORATION OF YOUR RELATIONSHIP WITH GOD?

Romans 8:38-39-For I am convinced that neither death nor life, neither angels nor demons, neither the present nor the future, nor any powers, neither height nor depth, nor anything else in creation, will be able to separate us from the love of God that is in Christ Jesus our Lord. (NIV Translation)

Write down a prayer, thanking God for always loving you and living inside of you. Say this prayer daily until this TRUTH is in your spirit.

_____

_____

_____

_____

_____

_____

_____

_____

_____

_____

_____

Daily Assignment:

- Write your Daily Affirmation on **My Powerful Affirmation's** pages in the back.
- Write down one thing you are grateful for and place in your **My Gratitude Jar.**

Day 7 Reflecting on My Truth

Congratulations!! You have completed your 8-week journey in search of your **TRUTH.**

Your Gratitude Jar should be filled to the brim, and whenever you have a trying day, read one of your powerful entries that you place in the jar. You'll immediately know that you have a lot to be grateful for.

You have also created a Powerful Affirmation List. On a Daily Basis, continue to go through your list and repeat them out loud. There is Power in Your Words.

For your final exercise, refer to your **My Powerful Affirmation** sheet. You gave yourself a Rate Number from 1-3 with 2 being "Kind of Living in My Truth and 3 being "Currently not living my Truth." Review the "2" and 3" on your list.

Has any of those rating changed to 1 "Living in My Truth" over the last 8 weeks?

Choose an affirmation that has most affected your life in a positive way and explain the steps you took to make the necessary changes.

_____

_____

_____

_____

_____

_____

_____

_____

_____

_____

_____

I want to thank you for taking this journey with me as we awaken your TRUTH.

Keep an eye out for "Living Your Blessed Life-Volume 2-Family Matters."

Justin A. Davis

MY THOUGHTS

MY THOUGHTS

Justin A. Davis

MY THOUGHTS

MY THOUGHTS

Justin A. Davis

MY THOUGHTS

MY THOUGHTS

Justin A. Davis

MY THOUGHTS

_____

_____

_____

_____

_____

_____

_____

_____

_____

_____

_____

_____

_____

_____

_____

_____

_____

_____

_____

_____

_____

_____

_____

_____

MY THOUGHTS

Justin A. Davis

MY THOUGHTS

_____

_____

_____

_____

_____

_____

_____

_____

_____

_____

_____

_____

_____

_____

_____

_____

_____

_____

_____

_____

_____

_____

_____

My Affirmations (Week 1-What's God's TRUTH about you?)

Wk1/D1-

_____

_____

_____

Wk1/D2-

_____

_____

_____

Wk1/D3-

_____

_____

_____

Wk1/D4-

_____

_____

_____

Wk1/D5-

_____

_____

_____

Wk1/D6-

_____

_____

_____

Justin A. Davis

My Affirmations (Week 2-Accept the TRUTH.)

Wk2/D1-

_____

_____

_____

Wk2/D2-

_____

_____

_____

Wk2/D3-

_____

_____

_____

Wk2/D4-

_____

_____

_____

Wk2/D5-

_____

_____

_____

Wk2/D6-

_____

_____

_____

My Affirmations (Week 3-The TRUTH shall set you FREE.)

Wk3/D1-

Wk3/D2-

Wk3/D3-

Wk3/D4-

Wk3/D5-

Wk3/D6-

Justin A. Davis

My Affirmations (Week 4-The TRUTH about the ARMOR OF GOD.)

Wk4/D1-

_____

_____

_____

Wk4/D2-

_____

_____

_____

Wk4/D3-

_____

_____

_____

Wk4/D4-

_____

_____

_____

Wk4/D5-

_____

_____

_____

Wk4/D6-

_____

_____

_____

My Affirmations (Week 5-Living God's TRUTH leads to PROTECTION.)

Wk5/D1-

_____

_____

_____

Wk5/D2-

_____

_____

_____

Wk5/D3-

_____

_____

_____

Wk5/D4-

_____

_____

_____

Wk5/D5-

_____

_____

_____

Wk5/D6-

_____

_____

_____

Justin A. Davis

My Affirmations (Week 6-Living God's TRUTH leads to WISDOM.)

Wk6/D1-

_____

_____

_____

Wk6/D2-

_____

_____

_____

Wk6/D3-

_____

_____

_____

Wk6/D4-

_____

_____

_____

Wk6/D5-

_____

_____

_____

Wk6/D6-

_____

_____

_____

My Affirmations (Week 7-Living God's TRUTH leads to PROSPERITY.)

Wk7/D1-

_____
_____
_____

Wk7/D2-

_____
_____
_____

Wk7/D3-

_____
_____
_____

Wk7/D4-

_____
_____
_____

Wk7/D5-

_____
_____
_____

Wk7/D6-

_____
_____
_____

Justin A. Davis

My Affirmations (Week 8-Living God's TRUTH leads to RESTORATION)

Wk8/D1-

_____

_____

_____

Wk8/D2-

_____

_____

_____

Wk8/D3-

_____

_____

_____

Wk8/D4-

_____

_____

_____

Wk8/D5-

_____

_____

_____

Wk8/D6-

_____

_____

_____

Printed in the United States
By Bookmasters